Time Alchemy:

The Art of Productive Living

Disclaimer

This Book has been written for information purposes only. Every effort has been made to make this Book as complete and accurate as possible. However, there may be mistakes in typography or content. Also, this Book provides information only up to the publishing date. Therefore, this Book should be used as a guide - not as the ultimate source.

The purpose of this Book is to educate. The author and the publisher do not warrant that the information contained in this Book is fully complete and shall not be responsible for any errors or omissions. The author and publisher shall have neither liability nor responsibility to any person or entity with respect to any loss or damage caused or alleged to be caused directly or indirectly by this book.

This Book offers information and is designed for educational purposes only. You should not rely on this information as a substitute, nor does it replace professional medical advice, diagnosis, or treatment.

Table of Contents

Introduction:
Understanding the Importance
of Time Management

Introduction

Understanding the Importance of Time Management

Time management skills are essential if you want to accomplish any task. Whether you want to improve your health, enhance your career, or complete short-term goals, you can't do so successfully without managing your time.

Do you have many goals but don't know how to reach them? You might feel too busy to accomplish important things for your lifestyle. Most people who struggle to find time to accomplish their goals feel overwhelmingly busy when they shouldn't.

What is time management?

So, are you wondering what constitutes effective time management techniques? You're not by yourself. One of the main issues individuals have, both personally and professionally, is managing their time well. Possessing good time management abilities indicates that you have the self-control to do activities quickly and stress-free.

The largest obstacle to having excellent time management skills is procrastination. People don't want to do boring things, yet in order to reach more ambitious objectives, you must do tedious chores. It's essential to have good time management skills to understand how long everyday chores take to finish.

Time management techniques

We'll talk about the several forms of time management you need to master before you go on your goal-attainment path. If you wish to complete things on time, different tasks call for distinct time management categories. People could approach sociability objectives differently from career-related goals, for instance.

plan

You need a strategy whether your objectives are long-term or short-term. To begin started, we advise making a concrete list of the things you aim to achieve. Otherwise, it might be challenging to make a to-do list that works for you. You should identify everything that stands in the way of your objectives during this planning phase. Next, make sure your list includes a strategy for overcoming that challenge. It would be challenging to finish crucial activities if you ignore obstacles.

Prioritize

Once you've written down everything you want to get done, you should prioritize your list by ordering your goals. Your top priorities should be those you can start working on right away or complete within the next several months. Prioritizing your objectives according to how important they are to your well-being is also very important.

Recall that after you embark on your trip, you may modify your list of priorities. When you prioritize these goals, you may find that there are obstacles you were unaware of. However, if you don't know where to begin, it might be challenging to reach the performance section.

Execute

Now for the challenging part. You've got your list of objectives and accomplishments, but now you need to tackle your to-do list. When implementing these goals, remember to take things one step at a time to make sure you're aiming for realistic time management successes. For instance, it's possible that some of the things on your priority list will take longer than you think.

Remind yourself that until you get up and do the task, it will not get done. Individuals frequently suffer from waiting for the ideal moment to form new habits. But if you're always making up reasons not to start a task, you'll never get started. Accept that there will never be a perfect moment, and work out how to modify your present plan to meet your requirements.

How your goals are affected by time management

Setting a deadline for yourself helps you stay on track with your goals. If not, you'll daydream about these objectives more than really pursuing them. You'll receive all you need sooner rather than later or never at all if you practice excellent time management every day.

Everyone has struggled with procrastination at one point or another. It's hard to get through the routine steps of fulfilling your desires, even if you have a desire in place. It's not feasible for people to get the benefits without making the necessary effort, although they would like to.

Take control of your time

However, some people find it difficult to develop their time management abilities because they believe they have little control over their surroundings or their time. It's simpler, for instance, to do tasks on your computer when your office is isolated from the rest of your home. When you are surrounded by individuals who are vying for your attention, working feels unachievable.

Having all kinds of distractions around you will make it hard for you to manage your time effectively. Even if it seems like you're simply taking ten minutes off of your assignment right now, those minutes add up. After working, wouldn't you rather unwind than become sidetracked?

Defining Your
Goals and Priorities

CHAPTER 1

Defining Your Goals and Priorities

After reading the previous section, it's safe to say you have a cohesive knowledge of time management skills. However, this knowledge can't take you far if you don't know what goals you want to set and how to start them. People subconsciously desire to improve their lives in several ways but often don't know how.

How to set goals for yourself

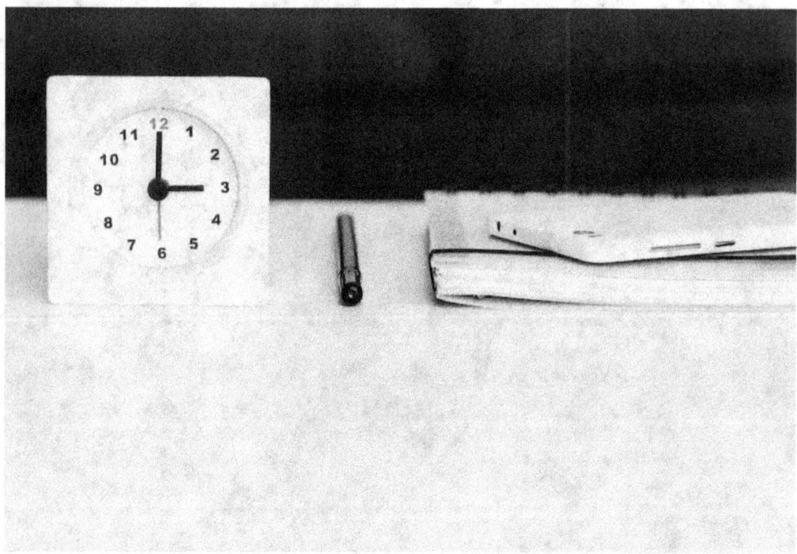

To decide which objectives you should work toward achieving, consider the aspects of your life that you would like to improve. If you're ready for the challenge, you may establish financial, professional, and personal objectives all at once. To avoid jumping in headfirst, it would be advisable to start modestly and pick one objective to concentrate on.

At the beginning of your paper, state your main objective. Next, set milestones for yourself by listing the tasks you must complete to reach your intended objectives. To keep oneself accountable, you should set deadlines for these accomplishments. It's simple to lose sight of your objectives when you don't assign yourself a deadline.

Identify problems as they arise

Most people run against obstacles in their path to their destination. But don't allow these setbacks to stop you from accomplishing your goals. If you ever want to make big changes, you have to learn how to work around business since it's a part of life.

As you go through your list of milestones, consider any issues that may arise and how to overcome them. Give yourself fifteen minutes to figure out why it's difficult for you to reach this goal and, if needed, modify the deadline.

List your goals from most to least important

Prior to selecting your objectives, make a list of the things in your life that you would like to change and rank them in order of importance. After that, you can group these objectives if you find that several of them are connected. For instance, while they may combine working out and exercising more, persons who want to achieve health-related goals might have different goals for each.

Though you are the only one who can determine their importance, objectives pertaining to your work or health are often more significant than recreational ones.

Therefore, if you believe that obtaining a hot tub is more important to you than being promoted, then prioritize getting the hot tub. Nobody can dictate to you which objectives should come first.

Identify your micro goals

There are generally several little objectives to complete in addition to the main objective when you have a big one in mind. To help you monitor your progress, we suggest designating these micro-goals as your milestones. Any action you do will result in a series of steps that you must take in order to get the desired results.

Let's look at some possible microgoals you can run across if you want to focus on the previously mentioned job promotion scenario. If you frequently arrive late for work, your manager is not likely to award you a raise or a promotion. Thus, being on time for work would be a micro goal for this bigger objective. After that, in order to do this, you'll need to plan your day. It's important to consider other variables impeding your objective of getting promoted once you establish the practice of arriving at work punctually. Do you find it difficult to interact, for instance, with coworkers? To get closer to your promotion, be willing to confront and resolve this possible issue.

Overcoming
Procrastination

CHAPTER 2

Overcoming Procrastination

Although it may sound absurd, one of the main things that might prevent you from achieving your objectives is procrastination. Completing a list of milestones may seem unachievable if you routinely put off work for as long as possible. You can still break the habit of procrastinating, even if you've battled it your entire life. Don't worry. Even among the world's most successful individuals, procrastination is a problem for them.

Knock out unpleasant tasks as soon as possible

People put things off because they are unwilling to do them. If an activity brings you joy, chances are you won't put it off. We advise completing tasks you don't want to undertake in order to avoid giving them too much thought. The worse disagreeable chores feel, the longer you think about them.

Attempt to finish the tasks you dislike doing first thing in the morning. One excellent task you may complete before tackling the remainder of your day is exercising. You're more inclined to skip exercising completely if you detest it and put it off until the very end of the day.

Use the Pomodoro technique

The ideal tool for procrastinators is the Pomodoro technique, which we shall cover in a later chapter. This method makes you concentrate on a single activity for an extended period of time. You will then return to work for 25 minutes after a five- or 15-minute break. Organizing your schedule in this way will assist you manage your routine tasks.

Get on your feet

You're less likely to push yourself to get out of bed and accomplish what you need to if you get out of bed and head straight to the sofa. In order to get your circulation flowing, try standing up and taking short walks around the house. Once your body is moving, your brain will function as required.

Even while it might be tempting to take a few minutes to relax before beginning your activity, it can take you many hours to realize that you've squandered your time. When you browse social media while relaxing, this issue is very apparent.

Set realistic expectations

When they establish new objectives, many individuals overestimate themselves. Remind yourself that you're not superhuman and that drastic adjustments to your daily routine never work. Regarding the amount of time and effort you put into your everyday chores, be realistic. To help you set realistic expectations, it might be useful to monitor your eating, sleeping, and socializing habits throughout the week.

By concentrating on your weekly routine, you may also choose which rituals you can replace with more goal-oriented activities and which ones you can keep. You'll have more time to accomplish your goals if you get rid of pointless routines from your day. Do you, for instance, spend hours perusing internet retailers in an attempt to save money? In this case, it's time to remove those shopping applications.

Establishing a Productive Routine

CHAPTER 3

Establishing a Productive Routine

It's easier said than done, everything. In order to overcome feeling overly busy and accomplish amazing things, you must modify your everyday routine.

You won't go anywhere if you spend your day feeling overburdened all the time.

It's time to establish a daily schedule for yourself that will help you reach your ultimate goal. Weight loss through daily exercise is a popular example of working toward a goal. In this case, your regimen might consist of regular exercise and your aim would be to drop 10 pounds in a few months.

Examine your daily rituals

Let's see what goes through your day. You first wake up and go about your daily activities in the morning, afternoon, and evening. Each person has a unique way of performing these everyday tasks. For instance, some people want a hot cup of coffee to begin their day, while others require a big glass of water.

Do you usually get your morning coffee at a drive-through? Alternatively, think about purchasing a coffee machine to enhance your financial objectives by saving money. A coffee maker will save you a lot more money in the long run, even if it costs more upfront.

On the other hand, you need to monitor your daily movement and food intake if you're trying to lose weight. Some find that wearing a smartwatch makes it easy to track their movement objectives. If you would want to be more aware of what you eat each day, there are applications that track calories as well.

Think about how everything you do during the day connects to your objectives. Of course, huge things don't always need you to alter your everyday routine. But you might be surprised to learn that even a small adjustment to your daily schedule might help you achieve your objectives. Furthermore, achieving these goals becomes concrete when you figure out how to organically introduce positive habits into your daily schedule.

Figure out what's getting in your way.

There will inevitably be obstacles in your path while attempting to build a productive habit. While some of these things are internalized, others are external. Don't allow these difficulties to derail you from achieving your goals.

As you progress through your routines, you will set little targets to help you overcome these issues. Are you attempting to develop the daily practice of preparing meals from scratch? You may find that your kitchen isn't set up for optimal performance as a workspace. Seek to enhance your surroundings so that achieving your objectives becomes easier.

Set morning and nighttime tasks

The manner you begin and end each day can have a significant influence on achieving your goals. You're setting yourself up for failure if you're the kind of person who sleeps in late and gets up early. Your body is set on autopilot by this habit, which causes you to feel occupied when you shouldn't.

You have a lot of things you want to get done that need you to get up early or at a certain time every day. Once you've finished your morning rituals, you'll have more time to fit goal-related routines into your day.

Before going to bed, you should also think about your evening routine. When they include relaxing activities like cleaning in their nightly routines, some people report feeling more productive. Consider how you might enhance your lifestyle by making little changes to your morning and evening routines.

Get on a steady sleeping schedule

People with irregular sleep habits are frequently those who feel too busy to achieve their goals. Establishing a regular sleep and wake time each day can assist you in developing a routine. On the other hand, you won't be able to provide yourself with an efficient routine if you operate with an erratic sleep pattern.

Sleep has a major influence on both physical and emotional well-being. Therefore, talking to a doctor about your sleep issues might help you get back on track if you're getting too much or too little of them. Additionally, prioritize your sleep pattern so that achieving other objectives will be simpler.

Set morning and night time tasks

The way you start and end your days can have a huge impact on goal achievement. If you're the type of person that wakes up late and rushes around in the morning, you're setting yourself up for failure. This practice puts your body on autopilot, giving you feelings of busyness where they shouldn't exist.

Many tasks you want to accomplish require you to wake up early or at a regulated time daily. Then, you'll be able to take your time completing your morning rituals and can incorporate goal-related rituals into your day.

You also need to consider your nighttime routine before bed. Some people feel productive when they incorporate cleaning or things that relax them into their bedtime practices. Think about how you can adjust your morning and night habits that can improve your lifestyle.

Get on a steady sleeping schedule

People who feel too busy to accomplish goals often have Inconsistent sleep schedules. Going to bed and waking up at the same time daily will help you establish a routine. Alternatively, if you work with a ragged sleep schedule, you won't have the mental clarity or physical ability to give yourself an effective routine.

Sleeping has a huge impact on mental and physical health. So if you're getting too much or too little sleep, speaking with a doctor about this problem could help you get on track. Also, make your sleep schedule high on your priority list so that accomplishing other goals is easier.

Learning to Focus and Eliminate Distractions

CHAPTER 4

Learning to Focus and Eliminate Distractions

When you're doing something you don't love, it's simple to become sidetracked. Because our minds are programmed to look for happiness and pleasure throughout the day, it's simple to become sidetracked when performing routine duties. You'll procrastinate as a result of these distractions, which will hinder your ability to perform well.

Many individuals consider themselves easily distracted, which may come as a relief. Therefore, you're not the only one who has learned how to get rid of these distractions in order to establish a productive workspace.

Put your phone away.

Cell phones are among the main sources of daily distraction for individuals. When engaged in an activity you're not enjoying, it's simple to lose track of time and scroll. Furthermore, a lot of apps may send you alerts that can cause you to lose focus on important work. Putting your phone aside while working might have a lot of advantages.

Regretfully, there are instances in which it is not feasible to put your phone aside. Some people must always have their phones close at hand in order to answer crucial calls while pursuing their objectives. Thankfully, there is a way to modify the do not disturb settings on your phone so that some calls can pass through.

Create a workplace

Creating a workplace that is specifically for your objectives is a terrific approach to go closer to achieving them. For instance, you should set up an office or office space in your house as your designated workstation if you have career-related ambitions. Alternatively, to make reaching your fitness objectives simpler, you should have an exercise area at home.

Your brain receives the message that these chores are not important when you don't set out a specific space to focus on them. If there are no distractions, you may set up a workplace without necessarily needing a separate room. If it works for you to accomplish your goals, your workstation could be as little as a nook.

Don't let others interrupt you

In social situations, it's simple to get carried away and let other people take you out of your work. For instance, it might be challenging to resist going out to dine with your friends at a bad restaurant if your objective is to lose weight. In this case, you may check the menu to see if there are any healthy alternatives, or you can arrange to meet up with your pals to go somewhere after they finish eating. Returning to the phone discussion, having your phone in your pocket makes it hard to concentrate on work. When you're just a text or phone call away, people tend to interrupt you more frequently. Please keep your phone usage to a minimum when working on critical projects that advance your objectives. If not, you will inevitably become sidetracked for a few hours.

Take scheduled pauses for yourself.

People occasionally think of themselves as powerful individuals capable of managing any work at any moment. This is an unreasonable expectation for your body and mind, though. Because of this, the majority of study strategies you come across incorporate breaks to prevent burnout.

You could lose interest in achieving a goal if you burn yourself out while working toward it. To avoid overworking yourself and losing interest in what you're attempting to do, you should schedule snack and lunch breaks throughout the course of your activity.

Timing these breaks wisely, though, is essential to effective time management. Otherwise, you risk going overboard. It will be challenging to return to the necessary job if you don't set a time limit for your breaks. When attempting to give yourself a break, you can set a timer on your phone or watch to help you avoid becoming obsessed with the ticking clock.

Delegating
Tasks Effectively

CHAPTER 5

Delegating Tasks Effectively

You'll come across some goal-related duties that you have to assign to other people. Let's take an example where your household's objective is to get cleaner. When working with a family, you have to make sure that each member contributes to the right chores.

You will burn out and the house will revert to its original condition if you attempt to clean it after everyone else as well as yourself.

To achieve this and other aims, assigning tasks to the right individuals is therefore essential to achieving your objectives.

Figure out your workload

Calculating the workload is the first step you need to do in order to assign assignments efficiently. Using the clean house scenario from earlier, let's go forward. Among the things to do in this case would be to take out the garbage, sweep the floors, and clean the dishes. To have a precise understanding of your workload, compile a list of all the things you need to do.

Deciding how much work you need to do will make it easier to delegate jobs to the right personnel. But, you could have more work than you anticipated, in which case you'll need to modify your tasks.

Establish timetables

Let's talk about how you'll fit these chores into everyone's schedules using the example of cleaning the house. You should talk to your family about how they can fit these duties into their regular routines and take into account the burdens they now face.

If you assign these jobs without first asking the appropriate individuals about their schedules, things might turn unpleasant.

For instance, a youngster will not have as much time to add additional responsibilities to their daily schedule if they are preparing for a final test at home. Thus, you should assign children shorter, less time-consuming chores, like putting out the garbage. On the other side, if you have a family member who is idle, you will have to assign them extra cleaning duties.

Assign the right people to the right tasks.

Make sure that the tasks you assign people are appropriate for their skill level and experience. Select the individual who's already departing for another assignment if you have someone who has to leave the house for that particular task. After that, they can pick up the object while traveling without obstructing the work of others.

Not everyone has the same mental hardwiring. While some people focus more on the small details, others have a broad perspective. A big-picture person should not be given work involving intricate details, and a detail-oriented person should not be given a big-picture task. Consider each person's advantages and disadvantages when assigning jobs to the right persons.

As soon as you have a mental inventory of everyone's strengths and current responsibilities, you may assign work as needed. To reach your goals, you don't have to carry the weight of the entire world. It's common to discover others who share your objectives and work toward them together.

Managing Stress
and Maintaining
a Work-Life Balance

CHAPTER 6

Managing Stress and Maintaining a Work- Life Balance

Reaching your goals becomes challenging if you stress about work during your leisure time excessively. This is the main cause of burnout and complete goal abandonment, particularly in the case of career-related ambitions. However, you'll go a long way and feel less busy if you manage your stress and maintain a healthy work-life balance.

Keep your personal and professional life apart by adhering to the advice provided here. When it's time to unwind, this exercise might help you achieve mental clarity and shift your focus from work. Taking breaks from your objectives is essential to stress management.

Reduce your at-home work discussion.

Imagine yourself wanting to chat with your family or friends about a hard day at work that you just got home from. This is typical! Before this talk, though, consider who your buddies are. You should find someone else to listen to your tirades if your friends or relatives are also coworkers.

Additionally, you don't want to talk about work all the time. Everyone gets frustrated at work from time to time, but dwelling on these issues makes it harder to move on. Sadly, your company will not pay you to ponder job-related matters outside of business hours, so now is the time to put such troubles to rest.

Establish limits with colleagues

People's desire to form friendships at work is normal. Working full-time allows you to develop relationships with coworkers and get to know them. Setting limits with these friendships is necessary, though, to prevent work-related issues from taking over your life. You shouldn't spend all of your time with your coworkers, no matter how much you care about them.

Additionally, avoid being available to them for conversations at all times. Refuse to answer on weekends if they know your mobile phone number so that you may give your personal life priority. It can become out of control to see individuals you already spend a lot of time with and communicate with them randomly.

Maintain the privacy of your personal life.

It might be tempting to gossip about your personal life with your coworkers while you're bored at work. Talking about certain things is acceptable, but you might wish to keep certain things private. Reduce the amount of time you spend discussing personal matters with friends, family, and love partners. People you work with shouldn't become interested in your personal details.

Generally speaking, you should also avoid having political conversations at work. The secret to keeping a healthy work-life balance is to keep your distance from your coworkers. Political conversations can become contentious and cause workplace hostility that you could be able to avoid.

Don't engage in work gossip

Talking about the newest rumors with your coworkers could be entertaining at first, but it can rapidly get out of hand. Individuals who engage in this gossip eventually find themselves on the receiving end of it, while abstaining from it lessens the conversation about you. Furthermore, talking at work might get you into serious problems and hinder your professional advancement.

It's advisable to quietly change the subject or leave the discussion if someone attempts to gossip with you while you're at work. Establishing this barrier will help you maintain a clear separation between your personal and professional lives and reduce stress linked to your work. If you stay silent, you won't have to worry about others finding out what you said about them.

Prioritize your hobbies

Of course, if you want to earn money and support your lifestyle, you have to show up for work. Money is a major priority since it serves as a driving force behind daily attendance at work.

Keep in mind that you do not live to work; rather, you work to live. Make time each day for activities you like doing to avoid feeling as though your only purpose in life is to get to work.

At the top of your list of priorities should be finding a pastime if you don't already have one. You may commit to trying something new once a week until you discover a pastime that you enjoy. Which activities you like and desire to devote your own time to may surprise you. Crafting, gaming, and TV viewing are examples of hobbies. Regarding how you use your leisure time, there are no rules.

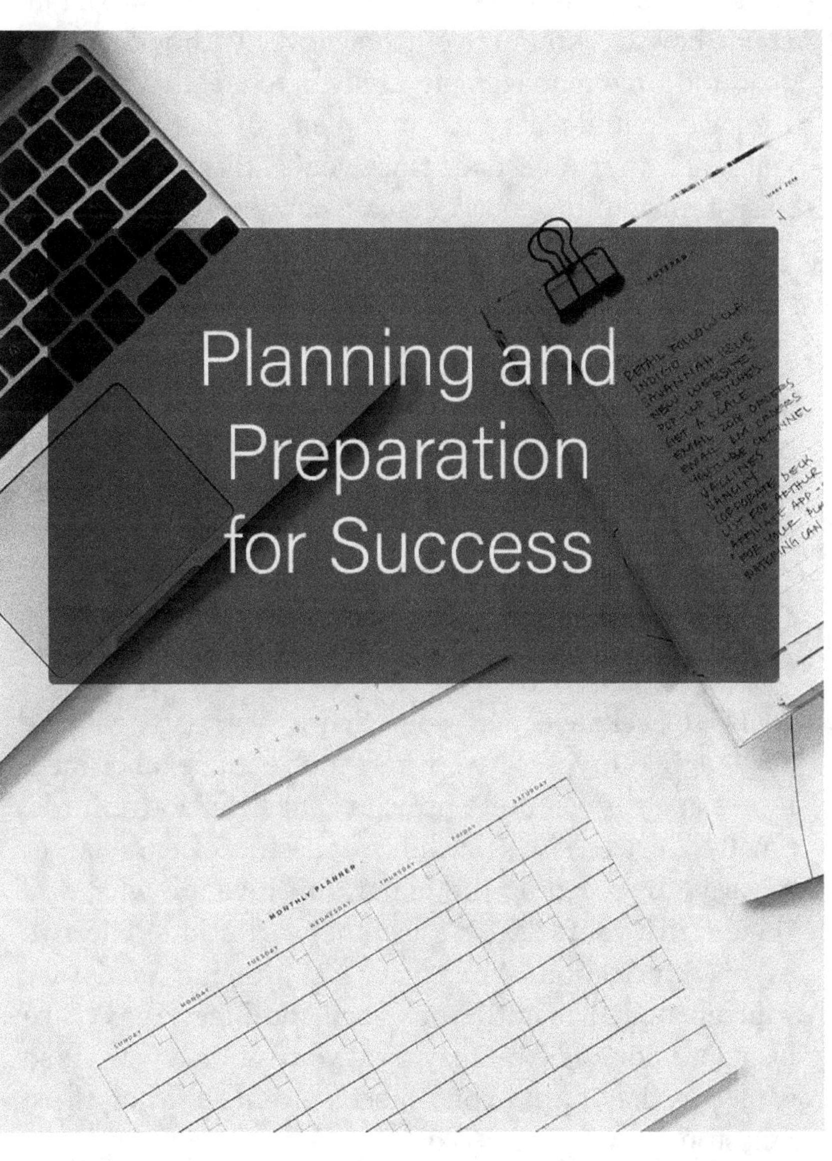
Planning and Preparation for Success

CHAPTER 7

Planning and Preparation for Success

Let's discuss your action plan with goals. Here, we'll talk about how to combine your objectives with your newly acquired time management abilities to create a win-win scenario. It's not necessarily the end of the road when you reach your objectives since you'll still need to strive to sustain your progress or create new ones.

For instance, you must stick to your new lifestyle if your goal is to drop twenty pounds. All of your efforts will be in vain if you return to the previous state of affairs after accomplishing this objective. This also holds true for objectives pertaining to your personal and professional lives. You'll eventually find it effortless to keep up your new routines.

Reward yourself

It's important to treat yourself when you reach your goals to acknowledge your hard work. It will be challenging to preserve what you've done and meet future goals if you don't provide your behavior rewards. Smaller prizes for reaching milestones and larger rewards for reaching the major objective are what you should give yourself. Let's use the weight loss objective as an illustration. You may set 5-pound goals for yourself to reach until you reach the bigger goal, like losing 20 pounds. You may treat yourself to a new video game or that outfit you've been eyeing during these milestones.

When rewarding yourself, though, make sure the benefits are in accordance with your objectives. Giving yourself a week off from eating healthily is not a good way to celebrate reaching your weight reduction target. This is ineffective and will cause you to revert to your previous behaviors. Instead, treat yourself to something else you appreciate that has nothing to do with your objective.

Figure out how to maintain your success

When you succeed, you must devise a strategy that will enable you to sustain your gains. If not, you risk losing all you've worked so hard for far sooner than it took to get it in the first place. The kind of goal you choose for yourself will determine how you keep it.

I'll take gaining a promotion at work as an example of a goal you should stick with for the time being. Your manager would probably demote you to your old job if, after receiving a promotion, you revert to a poor work habit. Then, it will be hard to get promoted again since your manager will recall how easily you revert to negative conduct.

On the other hand, your employer is more likely to offer you a promotion if you keep demonstrating to them that you're trying to increase your productivity. You don't have to stay where you began in your organization to advance through the ranks. To further advance your job and maintain this progress, you might set new goals for your work.

Prepare yourself for new tasks

It's only natural to set new objectives as you reach your current ones. People feel ravenous and are rarely content with their achievements. You should begin writing down your list of new objectives as you get closer to reaching the major milestone. But you don't have to jump right into these new objectives after finishing your old ones.

 After achieving your targeted goals, give yourself some time to enjoy and get used to your new lifestyle. If your aim was to buy a house, for instance, you might enjoy the enthusiasm for a while before focusing on home improvement objectives. You should celebrate your accomplishment—you just made a major life change.

Using the Pomodoro Technique for Maximum Productivity

CHAPTER 8

Using the Pomodoro Technique for Maximum Productivity

The Pomodoro technique was discussed in passing before, but because it works so well, let's talk about it in more depth. The Pomodoro technique can assist you in overcoming the issue of procrastination, diversions, or poor organizational abilities that prevent you from finishing projects on time.

Even if you don't have any problems with those, using this method to achieve your goals will make you more productive.

Whatever their objectives, everyone may gain from enhancing their productivity. Furthermore, this method is excellent for improving your time management ability

The Pomodoro Technique: What is it?

The Pomodoro technique is a useful tool for improving focus and attention span. You will use a timer to focus on one subject for twenty-five minutes, in order to use this strategy. Take a 5-minute rest when the timer sounds, then rinse and repeat.

Including a few 15-minute pauses would also be ideal, but this shouldn't be the norm. You may maintain your motivation by allowing yourself to take longer breaks to get food or leave your workstation. If you're working while hungry, you won't get anything done.

Examples of times to use the Pomodoro Technique

The Pomodoro technique may be used for a variety of objectives, however studying and school-related tasks are the most common uses for it. To get things done more quickly, try applying the Pomodoro technique when faced with an unpleasant task.

Depending on your line of work, you may apply the Pomodoro technique for cooking, cleaning, working out, or working. You may use the Pomodoro technique in countless ways to boost productivity and achieve your objectives.

How to combat procrastination with the Pomodoro Technique

Concentrating on your work might become challenging. A few individuals mentioned using the five-minute timer to help them feel like they have enough time to get ready before working. This is a useful strategy for overcoming procrastination and getting the desired outcome. Regretfully, if the tasks are necessary to achieve your objectives, you will have to force yourself to perform the unpleasant tasks. These routine jobs don't get done by themselves.

When to stop using the Pomodoro Technique

Once your objective has been reached, you can discontinue utilizing the Pomodoro technique. You should continue to employ this strategy until the end of the workday if you're utilizing it to stay productive. As an alternative, you may keep cleaning your house using this strategy until it reaches the degree of cleanliness you want. You will accomplish your objectives more quickly if you follow this method while working toward them.

There are, nonetheless, several circumstances in which this method is not applicable. The Pomodoro approach, for instance, is inapplicable nonsettings where regular breaks or steady concentration are required. In those situations, you'll need to come up with an alternative method for maintaining your concentration.

Turning Ideas into Action:
Strategies for Taking
Effective Steps

CHAPTER 9

Turning Ideas into Action: Strategies for Taking Effective Steps

You may believe that the most difficult aspect of reaching your objectives is planning ahead and arranging your ideas. Regretfully, your supposition is incorrect. We're only now beginning to tackle the challenging aspect of reaching our goals and getting over our sense of being overly occupied.

Anyone may make a list of things to do and goals, but carrying them out might be challenging. So, how can you put these aspirations out of your head and really start taking action? Well, you can help yourself with that by heeding the advice below.

Focus on realistic concepts

You have to be honest with yourself about your limitations when you create objectives for yourself. Sadly, there are certain objectives you'll have to postpone till you find yourself in a different circumstance. To get you closer to these seemingly unattainable big successes, you may, nonetheless, create smaller objectives and give them more importance on your priority list.

Living a sedentary lifestyle and hoping to wake up tomorrow with a brand-new exercise habit that you'll stick with forever is an example of an unreasonable ambition. It would be preferable to gradually introduce new fitness routines into your everyday schedule instead. Starting modest, such as getting in 30 minutes of exercise as soon as you get up, is a good place to start.

Get rid of obstacles

You must identify any obstacles before you can implement your ideas. Do you wish you could redesign your home, but you can't because of money? Prior to beginning your redecorating project, set budgetary targets for yourself.

As is always the case with new habits, you may run across difficulties. Before they start, it might be challenging for people to see the large picture and the minor obstacles in their path. To ensure that a barrier doesn't get in the way of your goals, you should record any obstacles you come across on your list of priorities.

Communicate with plan participants

Make sure you share your ideas with others if you have a goal you can't accomplish on your own. Finding others who share your objectives is a great way to include others in your goals. If you want to get more exercise, you might start a friendly competition with friends who also want to get more active.

If you're looking for people who share your aims, you can look for them by attending relevant community activities.

Connecting with like-minded individuals might be facilitated by volunteering, taking an exercise class, or attending financial seminars. Including people in your goals can assist you in keeping yourself responsible.

Set goals

Without objectives, it's impossible to create any kind of change in your life. Consider the aspects of your life or yourself that you would like to modify. You can set objectives based on the idea that there is always something you would like to get better at. Setting lofty objectives is not necessary if you want to change your way of living.

Organize priorities

Your list of objectives has some more significant goals than others, and they all relate to each other differently. As a result, you must order your priorities according to what is more desired and feasible than what is not. Yes, you may set lofty objectives for yourself that you want to accomplish in the future, but if they are unachievable at the moment, they ought to be lower on your list of priorities.

Start as soon as possible

It's not necessary to wait for the ideal time to begin working toward your objectives. You may begin accomplishing your objectives tomorrow, even though New Year's Eve isn't until a few weeks from now. Working for a healthy lifestyle doesn't have to wait until a specific day or hour.

 If you procrastinate too long, you'll probably forget your objectives and revert to your old routines.

 That being said, you don't have to begin with the most ambitious objectives on your list right away. You might begin by setting modest objectives, such as enhancing your morning routine or developing a productive sleep schedule. Long-term, major improvements will be easier for you to implement if you incorporate these organic modifications.

Measuring Your Progress
and Staying Accountable

CHAPTER 10

Measuring Your Progress and Staying Accountable

Monitoring your advancement toward your objectives may make a significant difference in your success. It will be challenging to accomplish the major milestones if you don't keep note of your smaller victories. To hold oneself accountable, you must rank the tasks you wish to do. You will never succeed if you don't believe that reaching your objectives is important.

Granted, there will always be instances where you have to give yourself some wiggle room, but this shouldn't become the standard. When you stray from your habit setting, you must immediately get back on track. One of the hardest parts of sustaining your development at these times is getting back up after them.

Create deadlines for yourself

Setting deadlines is the simplest approach to monitor your development and keep yourself responsible. Consider this: you would never complete a task if your employer never assigned you a deadline. The same idea holds true when forming new routines to accomplish objectives.

The dates you give yourself rely on the objectives you hope to accomplish. You may, for instance, set a goal for yourself to work out five times a week. If you haven't completed the workout before the end of the week, there will be no prize.

Break your progress up

Only little portions of more complex jobs can be handled by our thoughts. If you're working on a large project, you should divide it into smaller tasks. This might entail working on a task for a few hours every day until the desired outcome is achieved.

As an alternative, you may allow yourself some freedom by breaking your progress down into weekly chunks.

Looking at the broad picture too much might lead to feelings of overwhelm over your impending burden. You must break this work up into manageable chunks so that you may ease the burden on yourself.

Use a rewards system

Every time we strive toward a goal, our brains want to follow a reward system. To inspire further progress, you might give yourself tiny incentives each time you reach a goal.

If you make a mistake, a punishment-based system could deter you from reaching your objectives entirely, thus you shouldn't rely on it.

Punishing yourself for not reaching your desired objectives quickly will just make you feel less confident in yourself and further away from your desired outcome. You avoid letting your confidence erode and retain a good outlook when you design rewards for yourself.

Giving oneself a reward for good behavior encourages a positive outlook that moves you one step closer to success. Your brain will want you to keep doing these things because it will link this action to the reward you got. After you've treated yourself a few times, these new rituals won't seem like a bother.

Don't excuse your behavior

It's simple to rely on justifications for not completing the necessary chores. But ultimately, since it allows them too much latitude, people fail to meet their objectives. You have to be tough about your habits and make the necessary corrections along the way. That just means you have to identify and address issues rather than punishing yourself.

Making up justifications for why you can't accomplish your objectives just serves to further derail your intentions. Excuses such as "I was too tired" or "I was too busy" are common.

Just like you would with hand cleaning or tooth brushing, you must prioritize these new behaviors on a regular basis.

Try again and again.

To combat busyness, you may need to try your new behaviors several times until they become ingrained. If your first try doesn't work out, don't be too hard on yourself. Rather, use what you've learned from it and rework your strategy to give it another shot and strive for success. Analyze the reasons for the previous inability to accomplish this objective and devise a plan to overcome it.

It's hard to form new habits that last. Attaining your desired goals in life requires a great deal of self-control and pragmatic thinking. This self-discipline need is relevant to both professional and personal objectives as they both call for adjustments to lifestyles. When your body functions automatically, it might be challenging to recall your new behavioral habits.

Building and Maintaining
Positive Time
Management Habits

CHAPTER 11

Building and Maintaining Positive Time Management Habits

Lastly, if you don't improve your time management, it will be difficult to form new habits that will help you achieve your goals. We talked about time management before, but if you have trouble managing your time, we didn't provide you with many answers. Your time management abilities will improve if you adhere to the suggestions listed below.

Set a morning routine

Establishing a productive morning routine can help you achieve any objective you have in mind. Getting up and doing new things that aren't part of your routine is hard when you get out of bed. But when you haven't left your house yet, it's simple to start incorporating these new habits.

Getting up earlier than normal is the most difficult aspect of creating a morning routine. Your body isn't used to rising early, so the first few weeks will seem taxing. But once you become used to it, rising early becomes just another aspect of your day that you forget about.

If you find it difficult to get out of bed earlier than normal, try limiting this to a few weeks until you become used to it. Once you are at ease rising at the same time every day, incorporate more actions into your morning routine. To get your body moving, spend 30 minutes of that hour exercising rather than lounging on the couch.

By including duties in your evening routine, you may also simplify your morning routine. For instance, some people won't go to sleep if the dishes are still in the sink. They don't have to worry about the mess when they wake up because of this conduct.

Set reminders

You'll need to set a lot of timers and reminders for yourself when you first start your time management adventure. To receive reminders when you have tasks to complete, we advise adding these reminders to your phone's calendar app. You will no longer need to remind yourself of these routines once they become second nature.

To feel ready to take on the day, you can develop the practice of checking your reminders first thing in the morning. Set more reminders as needed throughout the day to ensure you don't overlook anything crucial. The fact that you may do without a physical agenda is among the greatest conveniences of owning a cell phone for everyone.

Making these reminders is an essential first step in developing a habit. You'll go back into your old habits if you don't remind yourself to complete new things. Even if you think of yourself as a disciplined person, it takes a lot of reminders to replace your old habits with ones that are beneficial to your lifestyle.

Create a schedule

Giving yourself scheduled daily routines can help you remain on top of your health and achieve your goals. Establish a flexible schedule that can be adjusted as needed throughout the day. For example, you'll still need to create time for last-minute plans with friends and family that will work for your schedule.

An example of creating a loose schedule would be planning your wake-up, meal, and sleeping times. You can add things to this basic schedule as you adjust. If you don't have a regular sleeping and eating schedule, then it could take a few weeks for your body to get used to this new behavior.

It'll be difficult to structure your day if you don't plan ahead. You're likelier to forget your daily goals without incorporating them into a schedule. The better you are at working on your habits, the more likely you are to achieve success.

Stay ahead of schedule

Unfortunately, unexpected circumstances can get in your way and make you late to events or set your plans behind. For that reason, we recommend staying ahead of schedule so you're ready for road bumps as they arise. Staying ahead of your tasks will help you avoid being late or feeling rushed throughout the day.

An example of an unexpected circumstance that could put you behind schedule is encountering a train on your drive to work. This common situation makes plenty of people late and irritates their employers. You can avoid this problem by leaving for work early, so traffic issues don't affect your arrival time. This practice will help you stay out of trouble in the workplace and in your personal life.

Attend to your needs

You can't build effective time management habits if you don't put yourself first. Neglecting your physical or mental health will make it difficult for you to accomplish your goals, which is counterproductive to our plans. Listen to your body and mind throughout the day to ensure that you don't burn yourself out.

One way to attend to your needs without neglecting your goals is to prepare yourself for potential hunger. Unfortunately, when you're working on yourself, it's common to forget about your snack times. You can bring portable goods with you to work or other functions, such as chips or granola bars.

If you're working with a busy schedule, you may need to plan out some naps throughout the day as well. When your body gets exhausted, it's hard to perform your best on essential tasks, but resting for a while could assist you with this problem.

No matter how extravagant your goals are or how busy your schedule feels, you must take good care of yourself. Everybody needs to rest once in a while, and it could be for a day or just a few hours. This rest includes not making social plans if you need a day to recuperate at home.

Adjust as necessary

The goals you start and the behaviors you develop could vary based on your lifestyle. Things cannot interrupt the daily routines that force you to look for other options. Your goals and the plans you make to achieve them are not set in stone. If you need to adjust, feel free to do so at any time.

Bear in mind that you are developing a new lifestyle to improve something about how you go about your life. If things don't work out as expected, you should not beat yourself up about it.

Instead, stay focused on your goals and change how you go about them.

For example, if you have the goal of waking up earlier and working out but you can't seem to make it stick, then you can adjust this change. You might feel better working out in the afternoon after you've already gotten out of bed and left the house. It would be better to work out at a different time than to give up your goal entirely.

Changing your goals and the way you go about them is a common method people employ when building new habits. When you're more willing to make these necessary changes, you increase your chances of achieving what you want.